OTHER TITLES

SET I.
WHEN GOD WAS ALL ALONE 56-1200
WHEN THE FIRST MAN CAME 56-1201
IN THE ENCHANTED GARDEN 56-1202
WHEN THE PURPLE WATERS CAME AGAIN 56-1203
IN THE LAND OF THE GREAT WHITE CASTLE 56-1204
WHEN LAUGHING BOY WAS BORN 56-1205
SET I LP RECORD 79-2200
SET I GIFT BOX (6 BOOKS, 1 RECORD) 56-1206

SET II.
HOW TRICKY JACOB WAS TRICKED 56-1207
WHEN JACOB BURIED HIS TREASURE 56-1208
WHEN GOD TOLD US HIS NAME 56-1209
IS THAT GOD AT THE DOOR? 56-1210
IN THE MIDDLE OF A WILD CHASE 56-1211
THIS OLD MAN CALLED MOSES 56-1212
SET II LP RECORD 79-2201
SET II GIFT BOX (6 BOOKS, 1 RECORD) 56-1213

SET III.
THE TROUBLE WITH TICKLE THE TIGER 56-1218
AT THE BATTLE OF JERICHO! HO! HO! 56-1219
GOD IS NOT A JACK-IN-A-BOX 56-1220
A LITTLE BOY WHO HAD A LITTLE FLING 56-1221
THE KING WHO WAS A CLOWN 56-1222
SING A SONG OF SOLOMON 56-1223
SET III LP RECORD 79-2202
SET III GIFT BOX (6 BOOKS, 1 RECORD) 56-1224

SET IV.
ELIJAH AND THE BULL-GOD BAAL 56-1225
LONELY ELIJAH AND THE LITTLE PEOPLE 56-1226
WHEN ISAIAH SAW THE SIZZLING SERAPHIM 56-1227
A VOYAGE TO THE BOTTOM OF THE SEA 56-1228
WHEN JEREMIAH LEARNED A SECRET 56-1229
THE CLUMSY ANGEL AND THE NEW KING 56-1230
SET IV LP RECORD 79-2203
SET IV GIFT BOX (6 BOOKS, 1 RECORD) 56-1231

the PURPLE PUZZLE TREE

It seems they learned a lesson, too,
about their mighty God,
and sang a song that's true:

    Our God is not a Jack-in-a-box
    But just as free as He can be.
    And you can learn what He is like
    From His great purple puzzle tree.

Which way do you think the cows went
when the ark was in their cart?
When the Israelites saw that cart coming,
they leaped and danced for joy.
They killed those cows
and held a mighty feast for God,
who sent His ark back home.

At last the long-legged Philistines
figured out a plan.
The priests of dopey Dagon
told them what to do:
"It seems the God of Israel,
this mighty Jack-in-a-box,
likes to send us rats and boils.
So let us make Him happy.
We'll take some gold and melt it down
and make five golden rats.
We'll take some gold and melt it down
and make five golden boils.
What do you think of that?

"We'll put them all inside the box
and put it on a cart,
pulled by two young cows.
The calves of those two cows
will be locked up in a shed,
bellowing for their milk.

"Now if the cows go off to Israel
and take the box back home,
we'll know it was their nasty God
who sent these rats and boils.
But if the cows come right back here
to find their bellowing calves,
we'll know that all this trouble
was nothing else but chance."

"The ark! The ark!"
the people yelled.
"That jumpy Jack-in-a-box.
That's the cause of all this trouble.
Send it off to another town.
Get rid of it! On the double!"

But in the next town
the very same thing happened.
The rats got worse!
And the boils got worse!

Next morning all the priests
came in to worship Dagon.
But they found him on the ground.
His hands were broken.
His head was broken.
His long, green teeth were broken,
and his orange eyes
were spinning in the dirt.

Then someone screamed, "The plague!
I've been bitten by a rat.
I'm breaking out with boils,
and very soon I'll die."

Our God is not locked up in His box
And blind to all your silly sin.
You cannot take Him out to war
To win and sin and sin and win.

In the fierce and filthy fight that day
the Philistines captured the ark
and killed the men of Israel
like weak, woozy flies.

They took the ark inside their temple
to their dopey god called Dagon.
He was staring at the ground
with dreamy orange eyes
and dirty, long, green teeth.

But the foolish men of Israel
took the ark from that high priest
and made up a funny song
from the words of cross-eyed Eli:

   Our God is not a Jack-in-a-box
   Who pops and stops and stops and pops.
   You cannot wind Him like a clock
   Until He stops and pops and stops.

   Our God is not Aladdin's lamp
   That gives you ev'ry wish you wish.
   You cannot swish Him with a cloth
   To swish a wish and wish a swish!

Then old cross-eyed Eli,
the great high priest of God,
told the men how wrong it was
to take God's ark to war.
"Our God is not a Jack-in-a-box
who jumps when you wind him up!
The ark is not like Aladdin's lamp
or a silly rabbit's foot."

Then some men said, "Ole!
Let's take the ark away!
If we take the ark to war,
God will have to fight for sure
to save His precious box."

Yes, the ark was a box
as big as a trunk,
covered all over with gold,
as bright as you've ever seen.

On the top there was a throne
where God would come
and speak to His high priest.
On the sides were cherubim
like two enormous lions
with fiery golden wings.
In that box were two stone tablets
that God once gave to Moses
on top of old Mount Sinai.

Then they started fighting,
and Israel sang the song of Joshua
as they often had before:

Now Yahweh will win this war for us.
Hurrah! Hurrah!
Now Yahweh will win this war for us.
Hurrah! Hurrah!
Now Yahweh will win this war for us.
He'll fight our foes and break their bows,
and we will win wherever Yahweh goes.

But this time it didn't work.
The Israelites didn't win.
For they didn't trust their God
the way that Joshua had.

The Israelites loved their new home,
that wonderful land of Canaan,
with olive trees and juicy grapes
and shining streams of water.

But then some enemies came
crawling over the hills,
killing cows, stealing boys,
and taking all the food.

The foes were a very funny kind
of long-legged, knock-kneed Philistines.
They had sharp, silver spears
but red, rolling eyes,
tall bronze shields
but hair that stuck out a mile.

How they laughed at the Israelites.
They laughed at their little spears
and they laughed at their little legs.
They laughed at their short swords
and they laughed at everything.

As Moses stood on a mountain looking at the Promised Land, he began to dream of God's garden of
love and laughter and a tiny tiger named Tickle. *The
Trouble with Tickle the Tiger* was that he didn't know
he was a very special piece of God's purple puzzle.
Now when the Israelites finally came to their promised
home, they found strangers there who wouldn't let
them in. So for 7 days they marched around the walls
of Jericho while the strangers laughed and laughed.
But on the seventh day, BOOOO-OOOO-OOOO-
OOOOM SPLAT! down fell the walls *At the Battle of
Jericho! Ho! Ho!* They loved their new home, but one
day some enemies came crawling over the hills and
they got scared. They didn't trust God to keep them
safe, so they tried to trick Him into fighting for them.
But He showed them that *God Is Not a Jack-in-the-
Box* who pops and stops when you tell Him to. And
because a little boy knew that, a giant man was killed
by *A Little Boy Who Had a Little Fling* with his sling
and one smooth pebble. This little boy loved God so
much that when he became king he threw a big circus
so all his people could praise God in a very happy
way. And God promised *The King Who Was a Clown*
that one of his sons would be the King of all men. The
next purple piece was Solomon, who was such a good
king that his people would *Sing a Song of Solomon*
to tell how good and fair and wise he was.
This is the third set in the Purple Puzzle Tree. In all
there are six sets with six pieces each; and when all 36
pieces are put together, they form the story of God's
plan for His people, from Creation to Pentecost. Each
of the purple pieces is recorded on a sing-along, read-
along, act-along record. If you listen with your heart,
you'll see God's love come alive through laughing
children's eyes.

Printed in U. S. A.   (ISBN 0-570-06516-X)   56-122(